McNamara

CW01623562

LangSyne
PUBLISHING
WRITING *to* REMEMBER

LangSyne
PUBLISHING
WRITING *to* REMEMBER

79 Main Street, Newtongrange,
Midlothian EH22 4NA
Tel: 0131 344 0414
E-mail: info@lang-syne.co.uk
www.langsyneshop.co.uk

Design by Dorothy Meikle
Printed by Printwell Ltd

ISBN 978-1-85217-330-2

McNamara

MOTTO:
Virtue and valour
(and) Strength in heaven.

CREST:
A naked arm, the hand grasping a scimitar.

NAME variations include:
Mac Conmara (*Gaelic*)
MacNamara
Macnamara

Chapter one:

Origins of Irish surnames

According to an old saying, there are two types of Irish – those who actually are Irish and those who wish they were.

This sentiment is only one example of the allure that the high romance and drama of the proud nation's history holds for thousands of people scattered across the world today.

It's a sad fact, however, that the vast majority of Irish surnames are found far beyond Irish shores, rather than on the Emerald Isle itself.

The population stood at around eight million souls in 1841, but today it stands at fewer than six million.

This is mainly a tragic consequence of the potato famine, also known as the Great Hunger, which devastated Ireland between 1845 and 1849.

The Irish peasantry had become almost wholly reliant for basic sustenance on the potato, first introduced from the Americas in the seventeenth century.

When the crop was hit by a blight, at least 800,000 people starved to death while an estimated two million others were forced to seek a new life far from their native shores – particularly in America, Canada, and Australia.

The effects of the potato blight continued until about 1851, by which time a firm pattern of emigration had become established.

Ireland's loss, however, was to the gain of the countries in which the immigrants settled, contributing enormously, as their descendants do today, to the well being of the nations in which their forefathers settled.

But those who were forced through dire circumstance to establish a new life in foreign parts never forgot their roots, or the proud heritage and traditions of the land that gave them birth.

Nor do their descendants.

It is a heritage that is inextricably bound up in the colourful variety of Irish names themselves – and the origin and history of these names forms an integral part of the vibrant drama that is the nation's history, one of both glorious fortune and tragic misfortune.

This history is well documented, and one of the most important and fascinating of the earliest sources are *The Annals of the Four Masters*, compiled between 1632 and 1636 by four friars at the Franciscan Monastery in County Donegal.

Compiled from earlier sources, and purporting to go back to the Biblical Deluge, much of the material takes in the mythological origins and history of Ireland and the Irish.

This includes tales of successive waves of invaders and settlers such as the Fomorians, the Partholonians, the Nemedians, the Fir Bolgs, the Tuatha De Danann, and the Laigain.

Of particular interest are the *Milesian Genealogies*, because the majority of Irish clans today claim a descent from either Heremon, Ir, or Heber – three of the sons of Milesius, a king of what is now modern day Spain.

These sons invaded Ireland in the second millennium B.C, apparently in fulfilment of a mysterious prophecy received by their father.

This Milesian lineage is said to have ruled Ireland for nearly 3,000 years, until the island came under the sway of England's King Henry II in 1171 following what is known as the Cambro-Norman invasion.

This is an important date not only in Irish history in general, but for the effect the invasion subsequently had for Irish surnames.

'Cambro' comes from the Welsh, and 'Cambro-Norman' describes those Welsh knights of Norman origin who invaded Ireland.

But they were invaders who stayed, inter-marrying with the native Irish population and founding their own proud dynasties that bore Cambro-Norman names such as Archer, Barbour, Brannagh, Fitzgerald, Fitzgibbon, Fleming, Joyce, Plunkett, and Walsh – to name only a few.

These 'Cambro-Norman' surnames that still flourish throughout the world today form one of the three main categories in which Irish names can be placed – those of Gaelic-Irish, Cambro-Norman, and Anglo-Irish.

Previous to the Cambro-Norman invasion of the twelfth century, and throughout the earlier invasions and settlement of those wild bands of sea rovers known as the Vikings in the eighth and ninth centuries, the population of the island was relatively small, and it was normal for a person to be identified through the use of only a forename.

But as population gradually increased and there were many more people with the same forename, surnames were adopted to distinguish one person, or one community, from another.

Individuals identified themselves with their own particular tribe, or 'tuath', and this tribe – that also became known as a clann, or clan – took its name from some distinguished ancestor who had founded the clan.

The Gaelic-Irish form of the name Kelly, for example, is Ó Ceallaigh, or O'Kelly, indicating descent from an original 'Ceallaigh', with the 'O' denoting 'grandson of.' The name was later anglicised to Kelly.

The prefix 'Mac' or 'Mc', meanwhile, as with the clans of the Scottish Highlands, denotes 'son of.'

Although the Irish clans had much in common with their Scottish counterparts, one important difference lies in what are known as 'septs', or branches, of the clan.

Septs of Scottish clans were groups who often bore an entirely different name from the clan name but were under the clan's protection.

In Ireland, septs were groups that shared the same name and who could be found scattered throughout the four provinces of Ulster, Leinster, Munster, and Connacht.

The 'golden age' of the Gaelic-Irish clans, infused as

their veins were with the blood of Celts, pre-dates the Viking invasions of the eighth and ninth centuries and the Norman invasion of the twelfth century, and the sacred heart of the country was the Hill of Tara, near the River Boyne, in County Meath.

Known in Gaelic as 'Teamhar na Rí', or Hill of Kings, it was the royal seat of the 'Ard Rí Éireann', or High King of Ireland, to whom the petty kings, or chieftains, from the island's provinces were ultimately subordinate.

It was on the Hill of Tara, beside a stone pillar known as the Irish 'Lia Fáil', or Stone of Destiny, that the High Kings were inaugurated and, according to legend, this stone would emit a piercing screech that could be heard all over Ireland when touched by the hand of the rightful king.

The Hill of Tara is today one of the island's main tourist attractions.

Opposition to English rule over Ireland, established in the wake of the Cambro-Norman invasion, broke out frequently and the harsh solution adopted by the powerful forces of the Crown was to forcibly evict the native Irish from their lands.

These lands were then granted to Protestant colonists, or 'planters', from Britain.

Many of these colonists, ironically, came from Scotland and were the descendants of the original 'Scotti', or 'Scots', who gave their name to Scotland after migrating there in the fifth century A.D., from the north of Ireland.

Colonisation entailed harsh penal laws being imposed on the majority of the native Irish population, stripping them practically of all of their rights.

The Crown's main bastion in Ireland was Dublin and its environs, known as the Pale, and it was the dispossessed peasantry who lived outside this Pale, desperately striving to eke out a meagre living.

It was this that gave rise to the modern-day expression of someone or something being 'beyond the pale'.

Attempts were made to stamp out all aspects of the ancient Gaelic-Irish culture, to the extent that even to bear a Gaelic-Irish name was to invite discrimination.

This is why many Gaelic-Irish names were anglicised with, for example, and noted above, Ó Ceallaigh, or O'Kelly, being anglicised to Kelly.

Succeeding centuries have seen strong revivals of Gaelic-Irish consciousness, however, and this has led to many families reverting back to the original form of their name, while the language itself is frequently found on the fluent tongues of an estimated 90,000 to 145,000 of the island's population.

Ireland's turbulent history of religious and political strife is one that lasted well into the twentieth century, a landmark century that saw the partition of the island into the twenty-six counties of the independent Republic of Ireland, or Eire, and the six counties of Northern Ireland, or Ulster.

Dublin, originally founded by Vikings, is now a vibrant

and truly cosmopolitan city while the proud city of Belfast is one of the jewels in the crown of Ulster.

It was Saint Patrick who first brought the light of Christianity to Ireland in the fifth century A.D.

Interpretations of this Christian message have varied over the centuries, often leading to bitter sectarian conflict – but the many intricately sculpted Celtic Crosses found all over the island are symbolic of a unity that crosses the sectarian divide.

It is an image that fuses the 'old gods' of the Celts with Christianity.

All the signs from the early years of this new millennium indicate that sectarian strife may soon become a thing of the past – with the Irish and their many kinsfolk across the world, be they Protestant or Catholic, finding common purpose in the rich tapestry of their shared heritage.

Meanwhile, many Irish clans and families proudly boast the heraldic device known as a Coat of Arms, as featured on our front cover.

The central motif of the Coat of Arms would originally have been what was borne on the shield of a warrior to distinguish himself from others on the battlefield.

Not featured on the Coat of Arms, but highlighted on page three, is the family motto and related crest – with the latter frequently different from the central motif.

Chapter two:

Hounds of the sea

A clan with a truly ancient and illustrious pedigree, the McNamaras trace a line of descent back through the dim mists of time from one of Ireland's earliest monarchs.

This is from Heber who, along with Heremon, Ir, Amergin and four other brothers, was a son of Milesius – a king of what is now modern day Spain, and who had planned to invade the Emerald Isle in fulfilment of a mysterious prophecy.

Milesius died before he could embark on the invasion but his sons, including Heber, Ir, Heremon and Amergin, successfully undertook the daunting task in his stead in about 1699 B.C.

Legend holds that their invasion fleet was scattered in a storm and Ir killed when his ship was driven onto the island of Scellig-Mhicheal, off the coast of modern day Co. Kerry.

Only Heremon, Heber and Amergin survived, although Ir left issue.

Heremon and Heber became the first of the Milesian monarchs of Ireland, but Heremon later killed Heber in a quarrel said to have been caused by their wives, while Amergin was slain by Heremon in an argument over territory.

Along with the McNamaras, other clans that trace a descent from Heber include those of Brady, Brennan, Carroll, Doran, O'Brien, O'Connor, O'Neill and O'Sullivan.

Adding further lustre to the McNamara pedigree is that they are recognised as being of the famed Race of Cas, also known as the DalgCais, or Dalcassians.

The Dalcassians were named from the legendary Cormac Cas, the early to mid-third century chieftain of the province of Munster who was renowned for his remarkable courage, strength and dexterity.

This progenitor of the McNamaras inflicted a celebrated defeat on the men of the province of Leinster in a battle fought near present day Wexford, but was killed in battle in 254 A.D. at Dun-tri-Liag, or the Fort of the Stone Slabs, known today as Duntrileague, in Co. Limerick.

His deathblow, according to the ancient annals, came from the spear of the Leinster king known rather colourfully as Eochy of the Red Eyebrows.

The McNamara, or MacNamara, name itself derives from a descendant of Cormac Cas known as Cumara, a chief of Maghadhain in Co. Clare, and whose name derives from 'Conmara', meaning 'hound of the sea.'

The first to adopt the 'Mac Conmara', or MacNamara, surname was Domhnall, a son of Cumara whose death is recorded as having occurred in the late eleventh century.

The dominant clan of the Dalcassian tribal grouping was the O'Briens, who take their name from the great Irish warrior king Brian Boru, and at whose side the McNamaras fought at the battle of Clontarf, north of Dublin, on Good Friday of 1014.

Late tenth and early eleventh century Ireland was the scene of vicious inter-clan rivalry as successive clan chiefs fought for supremacy over their rivals.

It was this disunity that worked to the advantage of the Norman invaders of the late twelfth century and the Viking invaders of previous centuries.

The period 795 A.D. to 1014 A.D. is known to Irish history as The Viking Tyranny, and it was largely through the inspired leadership of Brian Boru that Viking power was diminished, although not completely eliminated.

He was able to achieve this by managing to rally a number of other chieftains to his cause – although by no means all.

Among those who did rally to his banner were his fellow Dalcassians, the McNamaras.

Boru, also known as Brian Bóruma, was a son of Cennetig, a Dalcassian king.

With his warriors known as the Dalcassian knights at his side, Boru had by 1002 A.D. achieved the prize of the High Kingship of Ireland – but there were still rival chieftains, and not least the Vikings, to deal with.

These Vikings, known as Ostmen, had occupied and fortified Dublin in the mid-ninth century and had other important trading settlements on other parts of the island.

Resenting Boru's High Kingship, a number of chieftains found common cause with the Ostmen, and the two sides met in final and bloody confrontation at Clontarf.

Boru proved victorious, but the annals speak of great slaughter on the day, with the dead piled high on the field of battle, while hundreds of Vikings drowned as they sought the safety of their ships.

Among the many dead were Brian Boru's three sons, Murrough, Conaing and Moltha, while the king himself had little time to celebrate his victory – being killed in his tent by a party of fleeing Vikings led by Brodar the Dane.

The first to enter the tent had his legs cut off with one sweep of Boru's mighty two-handed sword.

Brodar then struck him a fatal blow on the back of his head with his axe, but he rallied the last of his dying strength to cut off his assailant's head with another sweep of his sword before killing yet another Viking.

Recognised as the second most powerful of the Dalcassian clans, the McNamaras had the honour of acting as the hereditary marshals of the O'Briens and, accordingly, officiated at the inauguration of the O'Brien kings of Thomond, in the northern reaches of the province of Munster.

County Clare was the stamping ground of the McNamaras, who eventually split into two septs located in West Clancullen, in the barony of Bunratty and in East Clancullen in the baronies of Upper and Lower Tulla.

The chief of the West Clancullen sept was known as MacNamara Fyne, with 'Fyne' derived from 'fionn', indicating 'fair' as in 'fair complexioned', while the East Clancullen chief was referred to as MacNamara Reigh, with 'Reigh' derived from 'riabach', indicating 'grizzled', or 'swarthy.'

Both septs of the clan became renowned not only as mighty warriors but also as builders of castles – erecting no less than 42 castles and 15 fortresses throughout Clare, including the imposing bastions of Knappogue and Bunratty.

On a rather more peaceful level, the McNamaras were also responsible for building a number of friaries, including one at Quin Abbey, near Ennis – where many of the name are buried.

But what proved to be the death knell of the ancient Gaelic way of life of native Irish clans such as the McNamaras was sounded in the late twelfth century in the wake of the Norman invasion of the island and the subsequent consolidation of the power of the English Crown.

English dominion over Ireland was ratified through the Treaty of Windsor of 1175, under the terms of which many Irish chieftains were only allowed to rule territory unoccupied by the Normans in the role of a vassal of the king.

This led to the creation through time of three 'separate' Irelands.

These were the territories of the privileged and powerful Anglo-Norman barons and their retainers, the Ireland of the disaffected Gaelic-Irish who held lands unoccupied by the Anglo-Normans, and the Pale – comprised of Dublin itself and a substantial area of its environs ruled over by an English elite.

Chapter three:

Raising Hell

Rebellion against the policies of the English Crown became endemic throughout the island, and it was in 1641 that a particularly bloody revolt erupted over the policy of settling, or 'planting' loyal Protestants on Irish land.

This was a revolt in which the McNamaras took part – an act for which they ultimately paid an expensive price.

The policy of plantation had started during the reign from 1491 to 1547 of Henry VIII, whose Reformation effectively outlawed the established Roman Catholic faith throughout his dominions.

This settlement of loyal Protestants in Ireland continued throughout the subsequent reigns of Elizabeth I, James I and Charles I.

In the insurrection that exploded in 1641, at least 2,000 Protestant settlers were massacred at the hands of Catholic landowners and their native Irish peasantry, while thousands more were driven from their lands to seek refuge where they could.

Terrible as the atrocities were against the settlers, subsequent accounts became greatly exaggerated, serving to fuel a burning desire on the part of Protestants for revenge against the rebels.

Tragically for Ireland, this revenge became directed not only against the rebels, but native Irish Catholics in general.

The English Civil War intervened to prevent immediate action against the rebels, but following the execution of Charles I in 1649 and the consolidation of the power of England's Oliver Cromwell, the time was ripe was revenge.

The Lord Protector, as he was named, descended on Ireland at the head of a 20,000-strong army that landed at Ringford, near Dublin, in August of 1649.

The consequences of this Cromwellian conquest still resonate throughout the island today.

He had three main aims.

These were to quash all forms of rebellion, to 'remove' all Catholic landowners who had taken part in the rebellion and to convert the native Irish to the Protestant faith.

He soon held Ireland in a grip of iron, allowing him to implement what amounted to a policy of ethnic cleansing.

His troopers were given free rein to hunt down and kill priests, while an estimated 11 million acres of land were confiscated and the dispossessed native Irish banished to the province of Connacht and to the ancient McNamara homeland of Co. Clare in the province of Munster.

An edict was issued stating that any native Irish found east of the River Shannon after May 1, 1654, faced either summary execution or transportation to the West Indies.

McNamaras were also among those who supported the doomed attempt between 1688 and 1691 to restore the deposed James II to his throne and, following his defeat in what was known in Ireland as the War of the Two Kings, a series of harsh penal laws were enforced against Catholics.

Some McNamaras, in common with other Irish Catholic families, took the reluctant but pragmatic step of converting to the Protestant faith.

Among them was a family whose most famous son still lives on in legend to this day throughout Co. Clare as John 'Fireball' MacNamara.

Born in 1750 at Moyriesk House, near Clooney, he was destined to become the black sheep of an otherwise respectable and law-abiding family.

His father was Colonel Francis MacNamara, a Member of Parliament in the British House of Commons for East Clare and a member of the Clare Grand Jury.

But John MacNamara showed signs from an early age of the fearless character he would later become – apparently receiving and accepting his first solid food as an infant from the point of a sword.

His family wealth enabled the teenage MacNamara to indulge in his passions of sport and general hell raising, his fiery and explosive temperament soon earning him the nickname of 'Fireball.'

Ever restless and in search of new adventures, he enlisted as an officer in the French Army – but it was not long before he had to flee French soil after fighting at least 30 duels that included killing two French officers who had been foolhardy enough to mock his Irish accent.

Serving as a military officer with the southern European states, he continued his duelling lifestyle and added to his growing notoriety as a skilled swordsman by also becoming a deadly pistol shot.

He even named his duelling pistols *Bas gan Sagar* – Death without a priest – while he also acquired another nickname of Sean Buidhe, or Yellow John, in reference to the tan he developed under the hot Mediterranean sun.

Returning to the family estate in Co. Clare, he continued his hellraising ways and, although raised a Protestant, supported the cause of Catholic emancipation.

This led to the loss of the estates he had inherited as chief of the MacNamara clan, while in 1798 he threw in his lot with the rebels in an abortive rebellion of that year.

The roots of the 1798 Rising are tangled in the thick undergrowth of Irish history, but in essence it was sparked off by a fusion of sectarian and agrarian unrest and a burning desire for political reform that had been shaped by the French revolutionary slogan of 'liberty, equality and fraternity.'

A movement had come into existence that embraced middle-class intellectuals and the oppressed peasantry, and if this loosely bound movement could be said to have a leader, it was Wolfe Tone, a Protestant from Kildare and leading light of a radical republican movement known as the United Irishmen.

Despite attempts by the British government to concede a degree of agrarian and political reform, it was a case of far too little and much too late, and by 1795 the United Irishmen, through Wolfe Tone, were receiving help from France – Britain's enemy.

A French invasion fleet was despatched to Ireland in December of 1796, but it was scattered by storms off Bantry Bay.

Two years later, in the summer of 1798, rebellion broke out on the island.

The first flames of revolt were fanned in Ulster, but soon died out, only to be replaced by a much more serious conflagration centred mainly in Co. Wexford.

Victory was achieved at the battle of Oulart Hill, followed by another victory at the battle of Three Rocks, but the peasant army was no match for the 20,000 troops or so that descended on Wexford.

Defeat followed at the battle of Vinegar Hill on 21 June, followed by another decisive defeat at Kilcumney Hill five days later.

Fighting in the thick of the battle of Vinegar Hill, MacNamara was shot and wounded in the thigh – and it is after this time that details of his subsequent fate become vague.

Some sources claim that he fled to England, where he was later hanged after being tried for highway robbery, while other sources rather more plausibly maintain that he lived out the rest of his days in the village of Quin, where he died in 1836.

It is certainly in the Lady Chapel of Quin Abbey, so dear to his ancestors, that he is buried – the spot marked by a Celtic Cross bearing the inscription: 'Erected by the Clan MacNamara to the memory of Sean Buidhe "Fireball" MacNamara, chief of clan and a 1798 Patriot.'

Michael Hogan, better known as the Bard of Thomond, also commemorates him in two poems.

These are *Fireball MacNamara's Address to his Pistols* and the moving *The Grave of Sean Buidhe MacNamara*, a verse of which reads:

Behold yon grey moss-covered stone
Where Thomond's maids shed drops of sorrow,
There sleeps Sean Buidhe – cold, low and lone,
The great and glorious MacNamara,
The heart and nerve that never shook,
The hand that left no mark unstruck.

Patrick MacNamara, meanwhile, is responsible for verse of a decidedly more upbeat note – for it was he who in the early years of the 20th century wrote the words for the rousing song *MacNamara, the Leader of the Band*.

Chapter four:

On the world stage

From acting and sport to politics and the field of battle, bearers of the McNamara name, in all its variety of spellings, have gained distinction in a wide range of endeavours.

Born in New York City in 1928, **Maggie McNamara** was the American actress who first rose to prominence in 1951 through her performance in a stage production of *The Moon is Blue*.

This led to her Broadway debut later that year in a production of *The King of Friday's Men*, while two years later she first appeared on the silver screen in a film version of *The Moon is Blue* – earning an Academy Award nomination for Best Actress and a BAFTA nomination for Most Promising Newcomer to Film.

Her second film role was in the 1954 *Three Coins in the Fountain*, and in the 1960s she appeared in a number of television shows that included *The Alfred Hitchcock Hour* and *The Twilight Zone*.

An actress with a troubled life, she later disappeared from public view and committed suicide in 1978.

In contemporary times **Brian McNamara**, born in 1960 in Long Island, New York, is the American actor who was nominated for a Golden Globe Award for Best Actor in a

Supporting Role for his part in the television movie *Billionaire Boys Club*.

He has also had film roles that include the 1990 *Arachnophobia*, in addition to guest roles in television series that include *Seinfeld*, *NYPD Blue*, *St. Elsewhere* and *Star Trek: Voyager*.

Born in 1965 in Dallas, Texas, **William McNamara** is the American actor whose film roles include the 1990 *Texasville*, the 2002 *The Kings of Brooklyn* and the 2005 *The Fallen*.

Best known for the creation and production of shows for television channels that include Disney, Cartoon Network, MTV and Nickelodeon, **Sean McNamara** is the American director, producer, screenwriter and actor who was born in 1962 in Burbank, California.

In the world of comedy **Dan MacNamara**, born in 1984, is the popular American comedian, artist and member of the comedy group the Upset Triangle, and who utilises special effects and video in his act.

Born in 1913 in London, **Caitlin MacNamara** was the wife of the Welsh poet and writer Dylan Thomas.

Portrayed by the actress Sienna Miller in the 2008 film *The Edge of Love*, she died in 1994.

In the world of music **Daniel McNamara**, born in 1979 near Bradford, England, is the lead singer of the British band Embrace, while his brother **Richard McNamara** is the guitarist.

Bearers of the McNamara name have also excelled in the highly competitive world of sport.

Born in 1886 in Randolph, Ontario, **George McNamara** was the talented Canadian professional ice hockey defenceman who played during the 1906-1907 season with the Sault Ste. Marie Marlboros of the International Hockey League.

He and his brother Howard, who also played for the team, were known as the Dynamite Twins, while another brother, Hal, was also a professional player.

Howard McNamara later went on to found the McNamara Construction Company, while George, who died in 1952, was inducted into the Hockey Hall of Fame in 1958.

Also in the world of ice hockey **Bob McNamara**, born in 1961 in Toronto, is the former goaltender who played for teams that include the Rochester Americans and the Milwaukee Admirals and who, at the time of writing, is general manager of the Grand Rapids Griffins of the American Hockey League.

On the tennis court **Peter McNamara**, born in 1955 in Melbourne, is the former Australian tennis player who won no less than five singles and 19 doubles titles throughout his career, while in baseball **Bob McNamara** is recognised as one of the oldest living men to have played in Major League Baseball.

Born in 1916 in Denver, Colorado, the former infielder played for teams that include Philadelphia Athletics.

On the fields of European football **Jackie McNamara** is the Scottish defender who was born in Glasgow in 1973.

A son of the Glasgow Celtic and Hibernian player Jackie McNamara Sr., teams he has played for include Dunfermline Athletic, Celtic, Wolves and Aberdeen, while at the time of writing he plays for Scottish club Falkirk.

He was also a member of the Scottish national team from 1996 to 2005.

Born in Boston in 1932, **John J. McNamara** was the American athlete who won a bronze medal for sailing in the 1964 Olympics in Japan.

Turning to writing after a period as an investment banker, his books include the 1967 *White Sails, Black Clouds*, the 1972 *The Money Maker* and *The Billion Dollar Catch*, published a year after his death in 1986.

Born in 1965 to Australian parents, **Julianne McNamara** is the former American gymnast who was not only the first winner, in 1984, of a U.S. women's individual gold medal, but who also has the rose Julianne McNamara named in her honour.

Bearers of the McNamara name have also gained distinction in the heat of battle.

Born in 1894 in Rushworth, Victoria, **Air Vice Marshall Frank McNamara** was an Australian recipient of the Victoria Cross – the highest award for gallantry for British and Commonwealth forces.

He had been a pilot with the Australian Flying Corps

during the First World War when, in March of 1917 in Egypt, he managed to rescue a fellow pilot who had been forced to land.

He later obtained the rank of Air Vice Marshall following the establishment of the Royal Australian Air Force in 1921, and during the Second World War served from 1942 to 1945 as Air Officer Commanding British Forces in Aden.

He died in 1961.

Also in the air, **Air Marshall Neville McNamara** is the former senior commander of the Royal Australian Air Force who was born in 1923 in Toogoolawah, Queensland, and who served as Australia's Chief of the Defence Force Staff from 1982 to 1984.

Yet another McNamara recipient of the Victoria Cross was **John McNamara**, born in 1887.

He had been a corporal in the 9th Battalion, the East Surrey Regiment, British Army, when in September of 1918 near Lens, in France, he helped to repel a German counter-attack on a trench.

He was killed in action only a few weeks later.

Also on the field of battle **Michael McNamara**, born in 1841 in Co. Clare and who later immigrated to the United States, was the U.S. Marine who was awarded the Medal of Honor for his actions during America's Korean Expedition of 1871.

He died just over a year after receiving his award for his

gallantry during the storming and capture of the Korean Forts.

In the world of politics and high statesmanship **Robert McNamara** is the former United States Secretary of Defense who was born in Oakland, California, in 1916.

Serving as Secretary of Defense from 1961 to 1968, a period that embraced the presidencies of John F. Kennedy and Lyndon B. Johnson and the Vietnam War, he later served from 1968 to 1981 as President of the World Bank.

His first wife was **Margaret McNamara**, who died in 1981 – only a few weeks after she was awarded the Medal of Freedom by President Jimmy Carter for her work in founding the Reading is Fundamental (RIF) programme for children.

The **Margaret McNamara Memorial Fund** was established in the same year as her death, with the aim of supporting the education of women from developing countries who are committed to improving the lives of women and children.

Also in the field of children's welfare, **Dame Annie Macnamara** was the Australian medical scientist whose contribution to children's health and welfare has been commemorated through a special Australian postage stamp.

Born in 1899 in Beechworth, Victoria, she died in 1968.

Also in Australia **Noel McNamara**, born in 1938 and along with his wife **Bev McNamara**, is a prominent campaigner for victims of crime.

It was following the murder in 1992 of their eldest daughter, Tracy, that they set up the Crime Victims Support Association.

They were awarded the Order of Australia (Companion) Medal in 2004 for service to the community.

In the ecclesiastical sphere **Archbishop Kevin McNamara**, born in 1926 in Newmarket-on-Fergus, was the Irish Roman Catholic academic and bishop who was an outspoken voice during the early 1980s on issues such as divorce and abortion.

Ordained as a priest in 1949, he served as Archbishop of Dublin from 1984 until his death in 1987.

To end on a contemporary and lighter note, one McNamara who has truly enjoyed the famed 'luck of the Irish' is **Dolores McNamara**.

Born in 1960 in Blackpool, England, but moving as a child back to her parents' homeland of Limerick, in the Irish Republic, this mother of six children and grandmother of four made history in July of 2005 when she scooped what, at the time of writing, is the biggest individual prize in European Lottery history.

Her winning numbers for the Euro Millions Lottery netted her a sum equivalent to over more than £91m, or $180m – making her the 72nd richest person in the Republic.

Key dates in Ireland's history from the first settlers to the formation of the Irish Republic:

circa 7000 B.C.	Arrival and settlement of Stone Age people.
circa 3000 B.C.	Arrival of settlers of New Stone Age period.
circa 600 B.C.	First arrival of the Celts.
200 A.D.	Establishment of Hill of Tara, Co. Meath, as seat of the High Kings.
circa 432 A.D.	Christian mission of St. Patrick.
800-920 A.D.	Invasion and subsequent settlement of Vikings.
1002 A.D.	Brian Boru recognised as High King.
1014	Brian Boru killed at battle of Clontarf.
1169-1170	Cambro-Norman invasion of the island.
1171	Henry II claims Ireland for the English Crown.
1366	Statutes of Kilkenny ban marriage between native Irish and English.
1529-1536	England's Henry VIII embarks on religious Reformation.
1536	Earl of Kildare rebels against the Crown.
1541	Henry VIII declared King of Ireland.
1558	Accession to English throne of Elizabeth I.
1565	Battle of Affane.
1569-1573	First Desmond Rebellion.
1579-1583	Second Desmond Rebellion.
1594-1603	Nine Years War.
1606	Plantation' of Scottish and English settlers.
1607	Flight of the Earls.
1632-1636	Annals of the Four Masters compiled.
1641	Rebellion over policy of plantation and other grievances.
1649	Beginning of Cromwellian conquest.
1688	Flight into exile in France of Catholic Stuart monarch James II as Protestant Prince William of Orange invited to take throne of England along with his wife, Mary.
1689	William and Mary enthroned as joint monarchs; siege of Derry.
1690	Jacobite forces of James defeated by William at battle of the Boyne (July) and Dublin taken.

1691	Athlone taken by William; Jacobite defeats follow at Aughrim, Galway, and Limerick; conflict ends with Treaty of Limerick (October) and Irish officers allowed to leave for France.
1695	Penal laws introduced to restrict rights of Catholics; banishment of Catholic clergy.
1704	Laws introduced constricting rights of Catholics in landholding and public office.
1728	Franchise removed from Catholics.
1791	Foundation of United Irishmen republican movement.
1796	French invasion force lands in Bantry Bay.
1798	Defeat of Rising in Wexford and death of United Irishmen leaders Wolfe Tone and Lord Edward Fitzgerald.
1800	Act of Union between England and Ireland.
1803	Dublin Rising under Robert Emmet.
1829	Catholics allowed to sit in Parliament.
1845-1849	The Great Hunger: thousands starve to death as potato crop fails and thousands more emigrate.
1856	Phoenix Society founded.
1858	Irish Republican Brotherhood established.
1873	Foundation of Home Rule League.
1893	Foundation of Gaelic League.
1904	Foundation of Irish Reform Association.
1913	Dublin strikes and lockout.
1916	Easter Rising in Dublin and proclamation of an Irish Republic.
1917	Irish Parliament formed after Sinn Fein election victory.
1919-1921	War between Irish Republican Army and British Army.
1922	Irish Free State founded, while six northern counties remain part of United Kingdom as Northern Ireland, or Ulster; civil war up until 1923 between rival republican groups.
1949	Foundation of Irish Republic after all remaining constitutional links with Britain are severed.